W9-BLL-812

The Mower

THE MOWER

NEW & SELECTED POEMS

ANDREW MOTION

With an introduction by Langdon Hammer

DAVID R. GODINE · *Publisher* · *Boston*

First published in 2009 by
David R. Godine, Publisher
Post Office Box 450
Jaffrey, New Hampshire 03452
www.godine.com

Copyright © 2009 by Andrew Motion

All rights reserved. No part of this book may be used or reproduced in any manner whatsoever without written permission from the publisher, except in the case of brief quotations embodied in critical articles and reviews. For more information, write to Permissions, David R. Godine, Publisher, 9 Hamilton Place, Boston, Massachusetts 02108.

LIBRARY OF CONGRESS CATALOGING-IN-PUBLICATION DATA

Motion, Andrew, 1952–
The mower : new and selected poems / Andrew Motion.
p.   cm.
ISBN 978-1-56792-389-6
I. Title.
PR6063.0842M68   2009
821'.914—dc22
2009001682

FIRST EDITION
Printed in the United States of America

Contents

Introduction
by Langdon Hammer

Andrew Motion's title for this book of new and selected poems – *The Mower* – reaches back in time to Andrew Marvell's mower poems from the seventeenth century. The reference is simultaneously nostalgic and wry, studied and casual. Motion is serious when he links himself to Marvell: this book determinedly takes its position in the long line of English pastoral poetry. But the mower in Motion's poem of the same title, placed last in the book and anchoring it, is not Marvell's imaginary swain and lyric singer. He is the poet's father, a stolid middle-aged man riding his roaring lawnmower in a weekend ritual that the poem remembers in exact, homely detail.

Motion wants us to feel the continuity between Marvell and Motion's own comfortable English childhood, but he also wants us to feel the distance between them. Both feelings come across in a finely rendered scene from *In the Blood: A Memoir of My Childhood* (which was published in Great Britain in 2006 and in the United States in 2007 by Godine). At this point, Andrew, who is sixteen, has just begun to read and write poems:

> I did most of my reading and writing outdoors. In the garden first, lying on one of the folding sun-beds dad kept in the garage, which had spiders living in the legs. As the metal heated up, the spiders escaped and crawled over my hands: pale sandy brown and light as a tickle. I brushed them off and went back to the poems of Andrew Marvell, which I'd bought second-hand [...]. While I was reading his poems about gardens, I gazed down the lawn towards mum's herbaceous border and

saw the words zoom off the white page like flies, vanishing into the laurel bush. It made me wonder how much I was understanding. Or how I was understanding, at least. Mr Way would have to explain.

The aptly named Mr. Way is a teacher who recognizes the teenager's literary gifts. He introduces Andrew to poetry and specifically to the poets who will determine his sense of vocation: Wordsworth, Keats, Hardy, Edward Thomas, and Philip Larkin. Poetry, defined by their examples, became for Motion a way to get closer to, but also to step away from and reflect on, his parents and their world.

The power of Motion's poetry depends on that ambivalence. It was already present in "the evening-mixture of sad and safe" that Andrew relished in the poems Mr. Way introduced him to. In Wordsworth, Hardy, and Thomas, that "evening" feeling is associated with the passing away of rural England. In Larkin, the nation's loss of empire and declining military power are added to the mixture. The feeling involves a turning away from modernity and modernization, but it implies for the same reason a specifically modern attitude. That attitude is central to the way in which modern English culture has tended to define Englishness. In this tradition, as it develops through Thomas and Larkin, moral realism and verbal precision, especially in description, balance the potential for vague idealism and naïve patriotism. Skepticism guards against self-pity. The irreverent and colloquial complicate romantic lyricism. Feeling is expressed through a carefully calibrated reticence.

Motion's poetry, from his first volume, *The Pleasure Steamers* (1976), to this book, his tenth collection of poems, in addition to his admired biographies of Keats and Larkin and his critical book about Thomas, strongly identifies him

8

with this tradition and its concern with English character and culture. So much so, it seemed inevitable to some commentators when Motion was chosen to be Great Britain's poet laureate in 1999. But Motion, as a resolutely private poet, was in some ways an unlikely choice for this public role, which is appointed by the monarch and tasked by custom with the writing of poetry for state occasions and events in the lives of royalty. When Larkin was asked to serve as poet laureate, he turned down the job.

Motion reflects on the relation between public and private life in a brilliant epigram reprinted here, "Mythology," an elegy for Princess Diana composed in 1997, before Motion became laureate. Here, in the second of two quatrains, the poet addresses the Princess:

> And you? Your life was not your own to keep
> or lose. Beside the river, swerving underground,
> the future tracked you, snapping at your heels:
> Diana, breathless, hunted by your own quick hounds.

Publicity literally takes the life of the Princess in this account of the car crash in which she died, pursued by paparazzi. Motion's terse title refers to both classical mythology and the contemporary worship of celebrity. By a clever stroke, he converts the Princess into Diana, goddess of the hunt, when her "own quick hounds" turn on her. In this grotesque version of the myth, the goddess herself suffers the fate of Acteon. Acteon is the hunter Diana punished for watching her bathe by turning him into a stag, who was killed by his own dogs. Motion's choice of "hounds" neatly holds the two ideas together – the hunting dogs and the news hounds with cameras; and the fact that these hounds are Diana's "own," and in that sense her pets, deepens the irony.

9

On another level, "Mythology" is a version of a story, based in experience, which Motion has told and retold restlessly in his writing, to the point that it has the status in his work of a personal myth. When Motion was seventeen, his mother fell from her horse while riding with the hounds in a fox hunt; she struck her head and, after surgery, entered a comatose state from which she never fully recovered before she died ten years later. *In the Blood* tells the story of her accident. The poems "A Dying Race," "In the Attic," and "Anniversaries," selected for reprinting here, deal with the ways in which Motion, his father, and his brother came to terms with Mrs. Motion's protracted suffering. "Serenade" observes the uneasy life, following the accident, of her horse.

Once we are sensitized to the force of the accident in Motion's imagination, we can feel the accident working indirectly in poems like "Mythology." "Anne Frank Huis," to choose another example, describes the house from which Anne Frank was taken away to her death. "Fresh Water" honors a female friend of the poet who drowned when a barge struck and crushed a much smaller boat, the *Marchioness*, which had been hired for a party on the River Thames. Our attention in these poems is on a woman's violent loss of life, but also on the poet's melancholy position as survivor and observer. In other poems, we can find other elements of the story. "The Fox Provides for Himself," for instance, is a virtuoso poem of animal description and imaginative sympathy. Here the poet and his wife watch a fox – the object of the hunt – slip into their yard and revel, at the end of the day, in a moment of perfect freedom and power. The fox tears at their children's punctured soccer ball, "bringing death down in a frenzy / of grins and delirious yaps." (The poem nods to Motion's predecessor in the laureateship, Ted Hughes, whose best-known poem is "The Thought-Fox.")

10

The Mower as a whole focuses less on Motion's mother than on his father. The first half of the book presents poems from Motion's earlier books, and "A Dying Race," placed first, as one of the earliest poems, brings the poet's parents together. Its title hints at an allegory in which the father in his pained tenderness and the mother in her wounded passivity represent the condition of a stricken people. But Motion does not insist on this reading. His concern is with a very private scene. The version of "A Dying Race" in this book is a revision of the poem as it appeared in *Selected Poems, 1976–1997* (Faber and Faber, 1998). Motion has condensed twenty-eight lines into nine, highlighting the final sentence, which remains the same in both versions (except for the pronouns: in the earlier version, it was "your hand" and "her desperate face," rather than "his hand" and "your desperate face"). What he discovers in the mute exchange is "the way love looks, its harrowing clarity." Or, that is what he wishes he "might have discovered by now" were he "still there": the sentence begins with "If."

"Harrowing clarity" is a stylistic ideal for Motion. "I want my writing to be as clear as water," he has said. "No ornate language; very few obvious tricks. I want readers to be able to see all the way down through its surfaces into the swamp." "All the way down [. . .] into the swamp": for Motion, surface clarity gives access to the darkness deep down. That play of surface and depth is the subject of one of the new poems in this book, "Diagnosis." It is one of the few poems here for which an American reader might need a gloss. Motion has set this meditation in the Orkney Islands of Scotland, so far north that there are "Twenty-one hours of daylight / now it's close to mid-summer." He describes his evening walks by the waters of Scapa Flow, the great natural harbor where, at the end of World War I, the German navy scuttled its fleet and, in World War II, a U-boat sank the battleship HMS *Royal Oak*. Motion watches the waves "slosh to and fro over the dead ships" and thinks of someone – a friend, a family member, his father? – who is living with a serious diagnosis, as if that figure could be seen "walking on the water." But the vision disappears whenever "the light shifts / and the sea beneath reveals itself again," reminding the poet and us that the "sea beneath" the surface is a grave.

The book closes with six poems about Motion's father. Suggesting a certain representative type of postwar British manhood, Mr. Motion is burdened and buoyed by his memories of military service, fatigued by the commuter train to London, irritated by "the new town simmering on the horizon," and fond of wistful country pursuits like fly-fishing. His diary is full of "pale blue empty pages," and his sons find him, though easy to love, "impossible to talk to." So it is fitting that he takes his "dying word" to the grave: his boys missed the moment of his death, we learn in "Passing On," when they stepped out of his hospital room for a drink at the pub.

Losing him, the poet feels the loss of the England that his father represented, as the latest in a series of pastoral figures stretching back to Marvell. The nostalgia in these poems is not simple, however. In "Veteran," when Motion prepares to go, at the end of the day, after a visit to his father, the old man leaves him with an ambiguous signal: "his slightly-lifted hand / either showing I should stay / or pushing me away." The double gesture of the old man's hand, expressing an essential ambivalence, belongs to the son as much as the father. Those mixed feelings have been present in Motion's poetry from the start, and are still at the center of it.

12

I · Selected Poems, 1976–2002

A Dying Race

I think of him driving south each night
to the ward where you keep on living.
I can remember the prairie-fields,

the derelict pill-boxes squatting
in shining plough. If I was still there,
watching his hand push back

the hair from your desperate face,
I might have discovered by now
the way love looks, its harrowing clarity.

In the Attic

Although we know now
your clothes will never
be needed, we keep them,
upstairs in a locked trunk.

Sometimes I kneel there
touching them, trying to relive
time you wore them, to catch
the actual shape of arm and wrist.

My hands push down
between hollow, invisible sleeves,
hesitate,
then take hold and lift:

a green holiday; a red christening;
all your unfinished lives
fading through dark summers,
entering my head as dust.

Anniversaries

The Fourth

Anniversary weather. I drive
under a raw sunset, the road
cramped between drifts, hedges
polished into sharp crests.

I have it by heart now;
on this day in each year
no signposts point anywhere
but east into Essex,

and so to your ward,
where snow recovers tonight
the ground I first saw lost
four winters ago.

Whatever time might bring,
all my journeys take me
back to this dazzling dark:
I watch my shadow ahead

plane across open fields,
out of my reach for ever,
but setting towards your bed
to find itself waiting there.

The First

What I remember is not
your leaving, but your not
coming back – and snow
creaking in thick trees,

burying tracks preserved
in spiky grass below.
All afternoon I watched
from the kitchen window

a tap thaw in the yard,
oozing into its stiff sack,
then harden when evening
closed with ice again.

I am still there,
seeing your horse return
alone to the open stable,
its reins dragging behind

a trail across the plough,
a blurred riddle of scars
we could not decipher then,
and cannot heal now.

The Second

I had imagined it all –
your ward, your shaved head,
your crisp scab struck there
like an ornament,

but not your stillness.
Day after day I saw
my father leaning
to enter it, whispering

If you can hear me now,
squeeze my hand, until snow
melted in sunlight outside
then turned to winter again

and found him waiting still,
hearing the slow hiss
of oxygen into your mask,
and always turning to say

Yes, I felt it then,
as if repeating the lie
had gradually made it true
for him, never for you.

The Third

Three years without sight,
speech, gesture, only
the shadow of clouds
shifting across your face

then blown a world apart.
What sleep was that, which
light could never break?
What spellbound country

claimed you, forbidding you
even to wake for a kiss?
If it was death,
whose hands were those

warm in my own, and whose
astonishing word was it
that day when leaving
your sunlit room I heard

Stay; stay, and watched
your eyes flick open once,
look, refuse to recognise
my own, and turn away?

The Fourth

The evening falls with snow
beginning again, halving
the trees into whiteness,
driving me with it towards

the end of another year.
What will the next one bring
that this has already abandoned?
You are your own survivor,

giving me back the world
I knew, without the years
we lost. Until I forget
whatever it cannot provide

I'll always arrive like this,
having no death to mourn,
but rather the life we share
nowhere beyond your room,

our love repeating itself
like snow I watch tonight,
which pauses on my window
then flounces into the dark.

Look

I pull back the curtains
and what do I see
but my wife on a sheet
and the screen beside her
showing our twins
out of their capsule
in mooning blue,
their dawdlers' legs
kicking through silence
enormously slowly,
while blotches beneath them
revolve like the earth
which will bring them to grief
or into their own.

I pull back the curtain
and what do I see
but my mother asleep,
or at least not awake,
and the sheet folded down
to show me her throat
with its wrinkled hole
and the tube inside
which leads to oxygen
stashed round her bed,
as though any day now
she might lift into space
and never return
to breathe our air.

I pull back the curtain
and what do I see
but the stars in the sky,

22

and their jittery light
stabbing through heaven
jabs me awake
from my dream that time
will last long enough
to let me die happy,
not yearning for more
like a man lost in space
might howl for the earth,
or a dog for the moon
with no reason at all.

Anne Frank Huis

Even now, after twice her lifetime of grief
and anger in the very place, whoever comes
to climb these narrow stairs, discovers how
the bookcase slides aside, then walks through
shadow into sunlit rooms, can never help

but break her secrecy again. Just listening
is a kind of guilt: the Westerkirk repeats
itself outside, as if all time worked round
towards her fear, and made each stroke
die down on guarded streets. Imagine it –

four years of whispering and loneliness
and plotting day by day the Allied line
in Europe with a yellow chalk. What hope
she had for ordinary love and interest
survives her here, displayed above the bed

as pictures of her family; some actors;
fashions chosen by Princess Elizabeth.
And those who stoop to see them find
not only patience missing its reward,
but one enduring wish for chances

like my own: to leave as simply
as I do, and walk at ease
up dusty tree-lined avenues, or watch
a silent barge come clear of bridges
settling their reflections in the blue canal.

24

The Letter

If I remember right, his first letter.
Found where? My side-plate perhaps,
or propped on our heavy brown tea-pot?
One thing is clear – my brother leaning
across asking *Who is he?* half angry
as always that summer before enlistment.

Then alone in the sunlit yard, mother
unlocking a door to call *Off so early?*
waving her yellow duster goodbye
in a small sinking cloud. The gate creaks,
and there in the lane I am running uphill,
vanishing where the woodland starts.

The Ashground. A solid contour swept
through ripening wheat, and a fringe
of stippled green shading the furrow.
Now I am hardly breathing, gripping
the thin paper and reading *Write to me.*
Write to me please. I miss you. My angel.

Almost shocked, but repeating him line
by line, watching the words jitter
under the pale spidery shadow of leaves.
How else did I leave the plane unheard
so long? But suddenly there it was –
a Messerschmitt low at the wood's edge.

What I see today is the window open,
the pilot's unguarded face somehow
closer than possible. Goggles pushed up,
a stripe of ginger moustache, and his eyes
fixed on my own while I stand
with the letter held out, my frock blowing,

25

before I am lost in cover again, *about the*
heading for home. He must have banked *pilot*
at once, climbing steeply until his jump
and watching our simple village below –
the Downs swelling and flattening, speckled
with farms and bushy chalk-pits. By lunch

they found where he lay, the parachute → *image of*
tight in its pack, and both hands spread *his body*
as if they could break the fall. I still *from their*
imagine him there exactly. His face pressed *imagination*
close to the sweet-smelling grass. His legs
splayed wide in a candid unshameable V.

tarte, in our own memories

26

To Whom It May Concern

This poem about ice cream
has nothing to do with government,
with riot, with any political scheme.

It is a poem about ice cream. You see?
About how you might stroll into a shop
and say: *One Strawberry Split. One Mivvi.*

What did I tell you? No one will die.
No licking tongues will melt like candle wax.
This is a poem about ice cream. Do not cry.

Hull

This is the park where Larkin lived
– moss-haired statues and dusty grass –
and a year or so after he'd packed and gone
     you lived here too

in one of those gaunt Victorian flats
where heat flies up to the ceiling and clings
in the intricate mesh of its moulding, leaving you
     frozen

whatever the weather, although it was freezing
in fact the day that I tried to persuade you
our life could go on, and we grappled for nearly
     an hour

on your hideous sofa (its bristling cloth
like tonsured hair which cannot grow back),
gasping, and gritting our teeth, and finally just
     giving up,

whereupon you plunged into your jersey again
and picked up a book, while I – pretending
nothing unusual had happened – went to the window
     and saw

a man in a belted mac returning from work
– a respectable man: brown glasses and trilby hat –
stop under one of the cavernous chestnuts,
     fling

his briefcase heavily into the branches,
crouch in a hail of conkers, chase them
hither and yon in the cobwebby shade,
     pocket them,

28

then disappear in the gloaming along with the others
you learn to expect in this fish-smelling pastoral:
home-going clerks, litter-bin lunatics, drunks,
    and those

who stand at their darkening windows and think
if they hurry there's time to get dressed and go out
and begin the day over again – with a visit, perhaps,
    to the plant-house

which glistens below, full of strangers who flounder
aimlessly round and round in its tropical bubble,
nod to each other through floppy-tongued leaves,
    and once in a while

stop at the cage where a moth-eaten myna bird
squats on its metal bough and says nothing at all
except – if you scare him badly enough –
    his name.

The Spoilt Child

It was a privilege to ride out
from the stables with his mother:
the world belonged to them,
they belonged to each other,

and the Labrador puppy slinking
beside them in and out of the hedge –
she belonged to them too;
she was part of the privilege,

trotting to heel just like that
as soon as the order came,
so all three seemed like mechanical toys
whose journey was always the same,

always began in the deep blackberry lane
softly, hooves cushioned on gravel,
then unwound gradually into the village
where mother and son appeared at window-level

trying hard not to stare in
through veils of variously figured lace
at lives they were happy to see lived
as long as each knew its place.

Here they never quite came to a halt,
only pretended they might be slowing
down sometimes for *Thank you; thank you –*
and now, really, we must be going,

before clopping on towards open country,
their minds filled with nothing,
or rather, filled with the thought
of lush meadows, hooves thundering,

and every horizon they might choose to face
splitting like water in front of a prow,
or splitting like earth itself
under the keel of a plough,

and going on splitting until –
as if it were dust striking his eye –
the boy saw a dog, a bull terrier,
apparently drop from the sky

and flatten the beautiful Labrador puppy
still trotting neatly at his side,
roll her so she was pale belly-side-up,
plant his bow legs astride,

and latch onto her neck. What comfort
then was his mother, shutting her eyes?
She might give her little scream,
she might cry,

but the outrageous teeth stayed locked
in the sleek golden throat,
and when the boy at last dismounted to look
they were bright shining wet

with the brilliant life-blood of his pet,
making him feel he was no use at all
no matter how he might thwack his whip
on the bull terrier's head, and call

for his beloved to rise up and fight,
and go on using his whip again, then again
and again, until at last giving way
when a stranger butted in –

a beery man wearing a vest,
and undone, down-trodden shoes,
who carried an all-metal hammer
and a stone he intended to drive through

the bull terrier's teeth to shatter them
if there was no chance of prising them loose,
which he decided at once there wasn't,
giving one, two, three steady blows,

with the pop-eyed boy watching
and the mother now covering her face,
before sinking down into his knees –
Jesus; Jesus; right then, in that case –

and finally hammering the stone
so far in, it stuck out the other side
of the terrier's foaming mouth,
opening it up wide

and leaving the puppy's neck plain
for the boy to see –
the pink windpipe, the oyster-coloured muscles
like a lesson in biology.

Sorry; I'm sorry, the mother and son
then thought they would hear the man say.
What they got was a single deep grunt
and a slow turn away:

It's all right, he said. *I'll deal with her now.*
It's all right. It's all right. Ah, but you see,
they thought, he was lying. Nothing was right
any more, nothing could change history –

and now, if nobody minded. . . ?
They set off home at the trot, and never looked round
once at the stranger watching them go, his dog in pain,
their own splayed on the ground.

Tortoise

Here is a man who served his generals faithfully
and over the years had everything shot away
starting from the ground and working upwards:
feet, legs, chest, arms, neck, head.
In the end he was just a rusting helmet
on the lip of a trench. Then his chin-strap went.

So he became a sort of miraculous stone,
miraculous not just for the fine varnish
which shows every colour right to the depths –
black, topaz, yellow, white, grey, green –
but for the fact it can move. You see?
four legs and a head and off he goes.

There's only one place to find the future now –
right under his nose – and no question either
where the next meal might be coming from:
jasmine, rose, cactus, marigold, iris, fuchsia
all snow their flowers round him constantly,
and all in their different ways are quite delicious.

It explains why there is no reason to hurry.
The breeze blows, the blossoms fall, and the head
shambles in and out as the mouth munches:
remorseless, tight, crinkled, silent, toothless, pink.
Life is not difficult any more, oh no: life is simple.
It makes you pause, doesn't it? It makes you think.

34

Fresh Water

in memory of Ruth Haddon

1

This is a long time ago. I am visiting my brother, who is
    living
near Cirencester, and he says let's go and see the source of
    the Thames.
It's winter. We leave early, before the sun has taken frost off
    the fields,

and park in a lane. There's a painful hawthorn hedge with a
    stile.
When we jump down, our boots jibber on the hard ground.
Then we're striding, kicking ice-dust off the grass to look
    confident –

because really we're not sure if we're allowed to be here.
In fact we're not even sure that this is the right place.
A friend of a friend has told us; it's all as vague as that.

In the centre of the field we find more hawthorn, a single
    bush,
and water oozing out of a hole in the ground. I tell my
    brother
I've read about a statue that stands here, or rather lounges
    here –

a naked, shaggy-haired god tilting an urn with one massive
    hand.
Where is he? There's only the empty field glittering,
and a few dowager crows picking among the dock-clumps.

Where is Father Thames? My brother thinks he's been
    vandalised
and dragged off by the fans of other rivers – they smashed
    the old man's urn,
and sprayed his bare chest and legs with the names of rivals:

Trent, Severn, Nene, Humber. There's nothing else to do,
so I paddle through the shallow water surrounding the
    spring,
treading carefully to keep things in focus,

and stoop over the source as though I find it fascinating.
It is fascinating. A red-brown soft-lipped cleft
with bright green grass right up to the edge,

and the water twisting out like a rope of glass.
It pulses and shivers as it comes, then steadies
into the pool, then roughens again as it drains into the valley.

My brother and I are not twenty yet. We don't know who
    we are,
or who we want to be. We stare at the spring, at each other,
and back at the spring again, saying nothing.

A pheasant is making its blatant *kok-kok*
from the wood running along the valley floor.
I stamp both feet and we disappear in a cloud.

2

One March there's suddenly a day as warm as May, and my
        friend
uncovers the punt he has bought as a wreck and restored,
cleans her, slides her into the Thames near Lechlade, and
        sets off

upriver. Will I go with him? No, I can't.
But I'll meet him in the water meadows at the edge of town.
I turn out of the market square, past the church, and down
        the yew-tree walk.

Shelley visited here once – it's called Shelley's Walk –
but he was out of his element. Here everything is earth
and water, not fire and air. The ground is sleepy-haired

after winter, red berries and rain matted into it.
Where the yew-tree walk ends I go blind in the sun for a
        moment,
then it's all right. There's the river beyond the boggy
        meadows,

hidden by reed-forests sprouting along its banks. They're
        dead,
the reeds – a shambles of broken, broad, pale-brown leaves
and snapped bulrush heads. And there's my friend making

his slow curve towards me. The hills rise behind him
in a gradual wave, so that he seems at the centre
of an enormous amphitheatre. He is an emblem of
        something;

somebody acting something. The punt pole shoots up
wagging its beard of light, falls, and as he moves ahead
he leans forward, red-faced and concentrating.

He's expert, but it's slow work. As I get closer I can hear
small waves pattering against the prow of the punt,
see him twisting the pole as he plucks it out of the gluey
    river-bed.

I call to him and he stands straight, giving a wobbly wave.
We burst into laughter. He looks like a madman, floating
    slowly
backwards now that he has stopped poling. I must look

like a madman too, mud-spattered and heavy-footed on the
    bank,
wondering how I'm going to get on board without falling in.
As I push open the curtain of leaves to find a way,

I see the water for the first time, solid-seeming and
    mercury-coloured.
Not like a familiar thing at all. Not looking
as though it could take us anywhere we wanted to go.

3

I've lived here for a while, and up to now the river has been
for pleasure. This evening people in diving suits have taken
    it over.
Everyone else has been shooshed away into Christchurch
    Meadow

or onto Folly Bridge like me. No one's complaining. The
    summer evening
expands lazily, big purple and gold clouds building over the
    Cumnor hills.
I have often stood here before. Away to the left I can see
    Oxford

throwing its spires into the air, full of the conceited joy of
    being itself.
Straight ahead the river runs calmly between boat-houses
before losing patience again, pulling a reed-shawl round its
    ears,

snapping off willows and holding their scarified heads
    underwater.
Now there's a small rowing boat, a kind of coracle below me,
and two policemen with their jackets off. The men shield
    their eyes,

peering, and almost rock overboard, they're so surprised,
when bubbles erupt beside them and a diver bobs up,
just his head, streaming in its black wet suit. There are
    shouts –

See anything? – but the diver shrugs, and twirls his murky
    torchlight
with an invisible hand. Everyone on the bridge stops talking.
We think we are about to be shown the story of the
    river-bed –

its shopping trolleys and spongy boat-parts, its lolling bottles,
its plastic, its dropped keys, its blubbery and bloated corpse.
But nothing happens. The diver taps his mask and
    disappears,

his fart-trail surging raucously for a moment, then subsiding.
The crowd in Christchurch Meadow starts to break up.
On Folly Bridge people begin talking again, and as someone
    steps

off the pavement onto the road, a passing grocery van,
irritated by the press of people, and impatient with whatever
brought them together, gives a long wild *paaarp* as it revs
    away.

4

Now the children are old enough to see what there is to see
we take them to Tower Bridge and explain how the road
     lifts up,
how traitors arrived at Traitor's Gate, how this was a brewery

and that was a warehouse, how the river starts many miles
     inland
and changes and grows, changes and grows, until it arrives
     here,
London, where we live, then winds past Canary Wharf

(which they've done in school) and out to sea.
Afterwards we lean on the railings outside a café. It's
     autumn.
The water is speckled with leaves, and a complicated tangle
     of junk

bumps against the embankment wall: a hank of bright grass,
a rotten bulrush stem, a fragment of dark polished wood.
One of the children asks if people drown in the river, and I
     think

of Ruth, who was on the *Marchioness*. After her death, I met
someone who had survived. He had been in the lavatory
     when the dredger hit,
and fumbled his way out along a flooded corridor, his shoes

and clothes miraculously slipping off him, so that when he
     at last
burst into the air he felt that he was a baby again
and knew nothing, was unable to help himself, aghast.

I touch my wife's arm and the children gather round us.
We are the picture of a family on an outing. I love it. I love
    the river
and the perky tour boats with their banal chat. I love the
    snub barges.

I love the whole dazzling cross-hatchery of traffic and
    currents,
shadows and sun, standing still and moving forward.
The tangle of junks bumps the wall below me again and I
    look down.

There is Ruth swimming back upstream, her red velvet
    party dress
flickering round her heels as she twists through the locks
and dreams round the slow curves, slithering on for miles

until she has passed the ponderous diver at Folly Bridge
and the reed-forests at Lechlade, accelerating beneath
    bridges and willow branches,
slinking easily among the plastic wrecks and weedy trolleys,

speeding, and shrinking, and silvering, until finally she is
    sliding uphill
over bright green grass and into the small wet mouth of the
    earth,
where she vanishes.

42

Goethe in the Park

The slates have gone
from that shed in the park
where sometimes the old sat
if they were desperate,
and sometimes the young
with nowhere better to fuck,

and now given some luck
the whole piss-stinking thing
will fall to the ground,
no, I mean
will lift into space,
without evidence left

in its earthly place
of the grey graffiti runes,
the deck of glue,
the bench with broken ribs,
where if things had been different
I might have sat, or you.

This moral won't do.
Think of Goethe who
all those centuries back
found a pure space like that,
his bench an oak tree trunk,
his view

a plain of ripening wheat
where retriever-dog winds
in a clear track
raced forward and back
laying a new idea at his feet
again and again,

again and again,
but not one the same,
until he was stuffed full
as one of those new-fangled air balloons
and floated clear
into a different stratosphere.

The oak tree stayed,
its reliable trunk
making light of the sun,
its universe of leaves
returning just as they pleased
each spring, so life begun

was really life carried on,
or was
until a lightning bolt
drove hell-bent
through the iron bark
and split the oak in two.

This moral still won't do.
You see
one crooked piece of tree
broke free,
escaped the fire, and found its way
into the safe hands of a carpenter.

This man, he liked a shed.
(I should explain:
two hundred years have gone
since Goethe saw
the future race towards him
through the wide wheat plain.)

44

That's right: he liked a shed.
He liked the way a roof
could be a lid,
and shut down heavily
to make a box,
a box which locked,

so no one saw inside
the ranks
of gimcrack bunks,
or heard things said
by shapes that lay on them
with shaved heads,

not even him.
He just made what was ordered,
good and sure,
saw everything was kept
the same, each nail,
each duckboard floor,

except, above one door
in pride of place
he carved his bit of tree,
not thinking twice,
into a face –
a merry gargoyle grimace.

This moral still won't do.
It's after dark,
and on my shortcut home to you
across the park,
I smell the shed
before I see it: piss and glue

and something like bad pears –
and yet,
next thing I know,
I've stepped inside it,
sat down on the bench
(it isn't pears, it's shit)

and stared up through
its rafters at the stars,
their dead and living lights
which all appear
the same to me,
and settle equally.

On the Table

I would like to make it clear that I have bought
this tablecloth with its simple repeating pattern
of dark purple blooms not named by any botanist
because it reminds me of that printed dress you had
the summer we met – a dress you have always said
I never told you I liked. Well I did, you know. I did.
I liked it a lot, whether you were inside it or not.

How did it slip so quietly out of our life?
I hate – I really hate – to think of some other bum
swinging those heavy flower-heads left to right.
I hate even more to think of it mouldering on a tip
or torn to rags – a piece here wiping a dipstick,
a piece there tied round a crack in a leaky pipe.

It's all a long time ago now, darling, a long time,
but tonight just like our first night here I am
with my head light in my hands and my glass full,
staring at the big drowsy petals until they start to swim,
loving them but longing to lift them aside, unbutton them,
tear them, even, if that's what it takes to get through
to the beautiful, moon-white, warm, wanting skin of you.

Glen Ellen Stories

for Roy and Aisling Forster

You must know already about Uncle Ollie
who drove here from England in a JCB.
Think of it jouncing across on the ferry.
Think of the tyre-tracks through Killarney.
Now he's the biggest big shot in Kerry,
grubbing up boulders and downing trees –
the dinosaur king of the whole county.

And I dare say everything known about Liz
long ago travelled beyond this parish.
How she blazed too bright in her Glory Days.
How her house split open and let in the sky.
Now she is living quite without gravity,
hauling herself each night upstairs
with a rope she somehow slung over a star.

And you'll also have heard about Des and Pat
who found new ways of murdering trout.
A dynamite stick tossed into the lough.
The massive catch of a water-spout.
Now Des is deaf as a sheet of slate,
and Pat just sits or ambles about;
he can't figure out where the profits went.

Which in the roundabout way of talk
brings me at last to the Mass Rock.
Real granite rock, but also a relic.
The secret altar the English wrecked.
Now where the Father did his work
buzz-saws chew up pines for matchsticks.
Go there, will you, and take a look.

48

Great Expectations

for Richard Holmes

I set my course south-east, and went to find
the Margate where John Keats – audacious, well,
and braced to catch the moment that his mind
became itself – hired lodgings like the swell
he never was, just off the central square –
then took the hairline track through wheat fields on
towards the clift (his word) and silence where
he saw Apollo step down from the sun.

I never got there. As I spun my way
through Kent, across the marshes, fog rolled in
so fast and penny-brown I went astray.
A gauzy church came next. Some graves. And then
a man in irons crouching by a stone –
exhausted, bloody-faced, and not alone.

On the Island

The intricate and lovely yacht we saw
was due to go,
that last night lay far out
and caught the sunset like a silver seed,

today has gone indeed
and left the skyline bare without a doubt,
except to show
we cannot think it saw us any more.

Serenade

There were the two ponies –
and there was Serenade, which belonged
to my mother. Though "who belonged"
would be better, in view of the girlish head-lift

she had, and her flounce to and fro in the lumpy field,
and that big womanish rump I always gave a wide berth to.
When the blacksmith came to shoe her, which was seldom
in summer but otherwise often, she would let him hoist

and stretch out first one hind leg, then the other,
with a definitely melancholy, embarrassed restraint.
The blacksmith was ferret-faced and rat-bodied,
hardly man enough to keep aloft the great weight

of one-foot-at-a-time, though he did keep it sort-of
aloft, crouched over double, and bent at the knees,
to make a peculiar angle which held each hoof still
on his battle-scarred apron. He would set up shop

under the covered entrance-way between
our house and the stable block: a ramshackle
clapboard affair, black (or black weathering to green)
with swallows' mud villages proliferating in the rafters.

I liked it there in the drive-through,
which was also where we parked the car (but not
on his days) – for the oil maps on the dusty concrete
brilliant as the wet skin of a trout, and for the puzzling

swallow-shit patterns, and most of all for that place
by the corner drain where a grass snake had appeared
once, an electric-green, sleepy-looking marvel
which, when it disappeared, left a print of itself

51

that stayed in the mind for ever. The blacksmith
always did cold shoeing, prising off each thin moon-
crescent, then carving the hoof with a bone-handled,
long-bladed knife. The miracle of no pain!

Serenade gone loose in her skin, her strength
out of her, so she seemed suspended in water,
her hypnotised breathing steady, the smell of piss
and musty hay and ammonia sweat coming off her,

her head dropping down, eyes half closed now,
and me a boy watching the earth-stained sole of her hoof
turning pure white as the blacksmith pared and trimmed,
leaving the nervous diamond of the frog well alone

but showing me, just by looking, how even to touch that,
much worse cut it, would wake her and break the spell,
and our two heads with it. Our collie dog sat near
where the snake had been, ravenous black and white,

all ears, sometimes fidgeting her slim front feet,
glancing away as if about to dash off, then twisting back,
licking her lips and swallowing with a half-whine.
She knew better than to get under anyone's feet,

but when the blacksmith had done with his cutting,
and offered a new shoe, and fiddled it downwards
or sideways, and hammered it with quick hits
which drove the nail-points clean through (but these

could be filed off later, and were) – when this was all
done, he kicked the clippings across the concrete
and now it was the collie's turn to show a sad restraint,
taking one delicate piece between her pink lips, ashamed

52

to be a slave of appetite, and curving away into the yard
to eat it, in private. The blacksmith straightened himself,
one hand smoothing the small of his back, the other picking
a few remaining nails from between his own darker lips,

then slapped Serenade on the flank with his red palm,
rousing her from her trance, running his fingers up
her mane and over her ears, giving each a soft tug
and saying *She'll do*, or *Good lady*, or *There's a girl*.

Whereupon my mother herself appeared to pay him –
their hands met, and touched, and parted,
and something passed between them – and the blacksmith
took off his apron with its colours of a battered tin bowl,

folded it, and carried it before him in a lordly fashion,
using it as a cushion for his collapsed bag of hammers,
clippers, knives, files, pliers and nails to the van
which he had parked in the lane some distance from us,

while my mother untied the halter and led her horse away.
There was a crisp clip-clop over the stable yard,
and a train of hoof-prints with the neat shoes obvious to me,
who had stayed behind with nothing better to do than look.

This was Serenade, who would later throw my mother
as they jumped out of a wood into sunlight, and who,
taking all possible pains not to trample her down, or even
touch her, was nevertheless the means to an end,

which was death. Now I am as old as my mother was then,
at the time of her fall, and I can see Serenade clearly
in her own later life, poor dumb creature nobody blamed,
or could easily like any more either, which meant nobody

came to talk to her much in the spot she eventually found
under the spiky may tree in the field, and still less
came to shoe her, so her hooves grew long and crinkled
round the edges like wet cardboard (except they were hard)

while she just stood there, not knowing what she had done,
or went off with her girlish flounce and conker-coloured
     arse,
waiting for something important to happen, only nothing
     ever did,
beyond the next day, and the next, and one thing leading
     to another.

A Glass of Wine

Exactly as the setting sun
clips the heel of the garden,

exactly as a pigeon, roosting,
tries to sing
and ends up moaning,

exactly as the ping
of someone's automatic car-lock
dies into a flock
of tiny echo after-shocks,

a shapely hand of cloud
emerges from the crowd
of airy nothings that the wind allowed
to tumble over us all day
and points the way

towards its own decay,
but not before
a final sunlight-shudder pours
away across our garden floor

so steadily, so slow,
it shows you everything you need to know
about this glass I'm holding out to you,

its white, unblinking eye
enough to bear the whole weight of the sky.

55

about Princess Diana [handwritten annotation]

Mythology

Earth's axel creaks; the year jolts on; the trees
begin to slip their brittle leaves, their flakes of rust;
and darkness takes the edge off daylight, not
because it wants to – never that. Because it must.

And you? Your life was not your own to keep
or lose. Beside the river, swerving underground,
the future tracked you, snapping at your heels:
Diana, breathless, hunted by your own quick hounds.

her death, escape [handwritten annotation]

seemed destined to happen [handwritten annotation]

Greek mythology [handwritten annotation]

fatalism [handwritten annotation]

so much has been said about her [handwritten annotation]

the stories yet to be told [handwritten annotation]

myths [handwritten annotation]

56

The Fox Provides for Himself

a couple

It could have been an afternoon at the end of our lives:
the children gone, the house quiet, and time our own.
Without a word, we stalled at a window looking down.

Weak winter sunlight sank through the beech tree next door,
skimming the top of our dividing wall, spilling a primrose
      stain
surprisingly far into our own patch. Earlier that same year

we had laid new grass, and the squares of earth underneath
      it all
still showed like the pavement of an abandoned town,
though the grass itself had done well, and from that angle

looked white as the breeze admired it, while we simply
went on standing there, holding hands now, trying to
      drown
the faint dynamo hum of London and lift off into nowhere.

Maybe we did drift a little. At any rate, something changed:
a shadow worked itself loose at the edge of our world.
Not a shadow. A fox. We saw it droop over the neighbouring
      wall

and step – using the sun as a plank of solid wood –
down through the air until, landing on all fours, it rolled
sideways (this was no stumble) and stretched out owning
      the place.

Big for a fox, I thought, but said nothing, holding my
      breath,
the sun burning so far into his coat each bristle stood
distinct, ginger everywhere but in fact red rising through
      brown

to black to grey at the tip, like bare plant stalks dying
towards the light, but of course soft, so I knew my hand
would come away warm if I touched and smelling of garlic.

First he lay there checking the silent earth with one ear,
but soon the music started and he was up – a puppet
living a secret life, stiff-spined but getting the hang of it,

imitating all that he had seen real foxes do and not been able,
examining leaves, staring out flowers, then deciding to stop
    that,
there was no danger here, only pleasure, and to prove it he
    must

fold his dainty front paws, stick his ramrod brush in the air,
angle his plough-shaped mask to the grass, keep his back legs
normal, and shunt himself slowly forward inch by inch,

left cheek, then right, then left, then right again,
smearing his mouth so far open I saw the pegs
of his teeth – the pink inside the gums flecked with black –

before he tired of that too, and found under our laurel bush
the children's football, a sorry pink-and-blue punctured
    thing
which must be killed now, *now*, and in one particular way –

by flicking it smartly into the air and, as it fell,
butting it almost too far to reach but hoiking it back
on invisible string, bringing death down in a frenzy

of grins and delirious yaps. After that, silence again.
When I returned to myself the fox was upright,
his coat convulsed in an all-over shrug

58

as if it were new and not fitting, like a dog when it jumps
out of water and stands legs braced in a halo of dew,
before trotting off in a hurry once more, which soon he did,

back to the neighbour's wall, and as he leaped he seemed
to hang on the bricks – slackened, to show his skeleton must
have somehow slipped from his body, or so I thought,

watching the breeze re-open his fur, and waiting to see how
he dropped – hardly a fox now, more like a trickle of rust –
my hand still holding your hand as he went, then letting go.

(the couple

observations, of the animal

59

In Memory of Elizabeth Dalley

The spring after Mervyn died
you sold the house and left
for the far side of the village –
a squat convenience cottage
your children all disliked
but you could call your own:

a garage-cum-deep-freeze;
a garden of dusty herbs
and purple heather clumps;
Constable skies beyond
a hedge-less prairie-field
the weather took to task –

whacking the wheat stalks flat
if it was their turn to show,
or polishing up the clay
to sickly yellow waves
when the tractor blundered in
trailing its cape of gulls.

Not that you had the chance
to follow a whole year through.
Almost the very day
things you chose to keep
were set in their final place,
and you stepped back to catch

the look of life alone –
plumped-up easy chairs
fattened to bear their weight
of leisurely widow-friends;
a print of Southwold beach
sun-sharpened in the porch –

the cancer which had been
caged up in Mervyn's life
burst through its brittle bars
and that was suddenly that:
the time you always planned
as a dawdling Indian summer

of soft-skinned cosy days
at home just sitting still,
or watching your rabbit-clan
play their games with age,
or planning a winter cruise
down old Galapagos way,

became the time to die.
Being the girl you had been
seventy years before
and never quite out-grown,
the girl whose soldier Dad
and pursed-up Scottish Mum

would sooner have had their teeth
yanked out than shed a tear,
you turned to stare it down
with the same unflinching gaze
as the moon in cloudless sky
above an ice-bound sea.

For instance: that autumn day
you ferried yourself to town
and bustled us off to lunch
in the new roof-restaurant
above Trafalgar Square –
where the National Gallery's dome

61

with its coat of feather-tiles
gleams like an osprey's head,
and Nelson at eye-level
perched on his coiled rope
(invisible from the ground)
shouts orders down Whitehall.

You stared without a word,
your head collapsed to rest
on the giant picture window,
with a dash of speckled sun
so bright across your face
it seemed you might already

have jumped the life to come,
seen the blaze of heaven,
and knew, which we did not,
that you would never again
set out to make a journey
as long and hard as this.

And after that, the months
spent hunting down a way
to match your dream of peace
with facts as they appeared:
the creature-claw of pain
scratch-scratching in your gut;

the lustre in your skin
a bogus bloom of health;
the squalid incubus
which hollowed out the rooms
and shining halls of you
then crammed them with itself.

To see you turn your hand
towards the simplest thing...
I mean that winter dusk
you made yourself go through
the kindness-chore of tea:
your sharp Formica table

stark with risky cups,
and the willow-patterned bowl
which suddenly flipped its lid
for no reason I could see,
to shatter against the tiles,
and strand us open-mouthed

in an aftermath of sound,
as though we'd heard the earth
accelerate through space,
and felt the silver whoosh
of moon and stars and planets
miraculously close.

I mean the way you found
the knack of how to match
a thought to words to speech
became mysterious.
I mean the hot delay
each morning in your bed

before you chose the clothes
which let you look the same.
I mean the strength to sleep
and then to keep awake.
I mean that strength run down
until each narrow day

had space for one thing less:
your pen a ton of steel,
the pages of the paper
slabs you could not lift,
the weakest sun too bright
to contemplate on us

who waited and who watched.
Watched, and saw the air
you left for us to breath
grow solid, then like water
close above your head,
and your life slip out of reach

to tumble through those currents
where the world eventually
wears down to simple rock,
then boulders, pebbles, stones,
then grains of shrinking sand,
then nothing we can see.

II · New Poems

On the Balcony

The other, smaller islands we can see
by turning sideways on our balcony –

the bubble-pods and cones, the flecks of green,
the basalt-prongs, the moles, the lumpy chains –

were all volcanoes once, though none so tall
and full of rage for life as ours, which still

displays its flag of supple, wind-stirred smoke
as proof that one day soon it will awake

again and wave its swizzle-stick of fire,
demolish woods, block roads, consume entire

communities with stinking lava-slews
which seem too prehistoric to be true

but are. Or will be. For today we sit
and feel what happiness the world permits.

The metal sun hangs still, its shadows fixed
and permanent. The sea-smell mixed

with thyme and oleander throws a drape
insidious as mist across the drop

of roofs and aerials, of jigsaw squares,
of terraced streets side-stepping to the shore,

of bathers sprawling on their stones, of waves
like other bathers turning in their graves,

and there, beyond them in the blistered shade
below the mountain, of the clumsy bird –

no, bi-plane, with a bucket slung beneath –
which sidles idly in to drench a wreath

of bush-fire in the fields, a fire that we
suppose means nothing to us here, but have to see.

Harry Patch

"The Last Fighting Tommy"

I.

A curve is a straight line caught bending
and this one runs under the kitchen window
where the bright eyes of your mum and dad
might flash any minute and find you down
on all fours, stomach hard to the ground,
slinking along a furrow between the potatoes
and dead set on a prospect of rich pickings,
the good apple trees and plum trees and pears,
anything sweet and juicy you might now be
able to nibble round the back and leave
hanging as though nothing had touched it,
if only it were possible to stand upright
in so much clear light with those eyes
beady in the window and not catch a packet.

II.

Patch, Harry Patch, that's a good name,
Shakespearean, it might be one of Hal's men
at Agincourt or not far off, although in fact
it starts life and belongs in Combe Down
with your dad's trade in the canary limestone
which turns to grey and hardens when it meets
the light, perfect for Regency Bath and you too
since no one these days thinks about the danger
of playing in quarries when the workmen go,
not even of prodding and pelting with stones
the wasps' nests perched on rough ledges
or dropped down from the ceiling on stalks
although god knows it means having to shift
tout de suite and still get stung on arms and faces.

III.

First the hard facts of not wanting to fight,
and the kindness of deciding to shoot men
in the legs but no higher unless needs must,
and the liking among comrades which is truly
as deep as love without that particular name,
then Pilckem Ridge and Langemarck and across
the Steenbeek since none of the above can change
what comes next, which is a lad from A Company
shrapnel has ripped open from shoulder to waist
who begs you "Shoot me," but is good as dead
already, and whose final word is "Mother,"
which you hear because you kneel a minute,
hold one finger of his hand, then remember orders
to keep pressing on, support the infantry ahead.

IV.

After the beautiful crowd to unveil the memorial
and no puff in the lungs to sing "O Valiant Hearts"
or say aloud the names of friends and one cousin,
the butcher and chimney sweep, a farmer, a carpenter,
work comes up the Wills Tower in Bristol and there
thunderstorms are a danger, so bad that lightning
one day hammers Great George and knocks down
the foreman who can't use his hand three weeks
later as you recall, along with the way that strike
burned all trace of oxygen from the air, it must have,
given the definite stink of sulphur and a second
or two later the shy wave of a breeze returning
along with rooftops below, and moss, and rain
fading the green Mendip Hills and blue Severn.

V.

You grow a moustache, check the mirror, notice
you're forty years old, then next day shave it off,
check the mirror again – and find you're seventy,
but life is like that now, suddenly and gradually
everyone you know dies and still comes to visit
or you head back to them, it's not clear which
only where it happens: a safe bedroom upstairs
on the face of it, although when you sit late
whispering with the other boys in the Lewis team,
smoking your pipe upside-down to hide the fire,
and the nurses on night duty bring folded sheets
to store in the linen cupboard opposite, all it takes
is someone switching on the light – there is that flash,
or was until you said, and the staff blacked the window.

The Feather Pole

Today comes from the Netherlands
for some unknown reason my remaindered
Oxford Dictionary of British Bird Names.

Bush Oven I am pleased to discover is a *Norfolk*
variant for the Long-Tailed Tit, but properly
the intricate and dome-shaped nest here likened

to an oven. I could get used to that. As I could also
come to like the Feather Pole, and other words
describing nests but actually the bird.

The Life of William Cowper

Balloons are so much the mode, even in the country
we have attempted one. You may remember at Weston,
little more than a mile from Olney, there now lives
a family whose name is Throckmorton. They are Papists,
but more amiable than many Protestants hereabouts.

Mrs Unwin, your mother, and I have no close connection
with them, though ever since living here we have enjoyed
the range of their pleasure-grounds, having been favoured
with the courtesy of a key. The present possessor of the estate
is a young man whom I remember well as a child-in-arms,

and when he succeeded I sent him a complimentary card,
requesting the continuance of our privilege. He granted it,
and nothing more passed between us. Then, a fortnight ago,
I received from him an invitation, in which I understood
that next day they would attempt to fill the balloon and be

happy to see me. Your mother and I went. The whole country
was there, but the balloon would not be filled. Indeed, it lay
all afternoon on the grass and refused every encouragement.
The process, I believe, depends for its success upon niceties
as make it very precarious. Our own reception was, however,

flattering to a degree, insomuch that more notice was taken
of us than we could possibly have expected. Our kind hosts
even seemed anxious to recommend themselves to our
        regards.
We drank chocolate and were asked to dine, but were
        engaged.
This happened a week ago. To the best of my knowledge

no further plan has been made to inflate the balloon,
    although
I admit not a day has passed without my wishing either
    for it
to be in the heavens above my head, or else become the
    means
of my looking down upon the earth beneath. And so
    farewell.
I have told you a long story. We number the days as they
    pass.

My Masterpiece

In my other life
I am the darling
of the high Renaissance,

and have just completed
my consummate masterpiece
"Madonna in a Window."

The compassion of the face
and unknowable frown
are both conundrums

which will outwit scholars
and bewitch the public
for the rest of time.

But my real triumph
consists in the view
extending behind her,

the mile upon mile
of blue-green hills
with their miniature lives.

That miller for instance
who shuts up shop
at the height of harvest

and all for a carp
like a flake of gold
in the stream by his wheel.

Or this poacher-boy
who checked his snare
but discovered instead

his bare-headed girl
with time to kill
in a cypress grove.

The lovely Madonna –
I already know
the depth of her secret;

theirs escapes me,
in much the same way
that a perilous sun-shaft

flees through a landscape
and just for a second
fulfils what it strikes

before galleon clouds
storm in behind it
and drop their anchors.

Migration

On the hard standing below the top field
where the slope ends in a water meadow
and the canal beside two dogs playing,
an articulated lorry has come to rest –
its cab gone and the green metal container
open like the first sentence in a long story.

No footprints on the asphalt or the towpath,
but yellow leaves streaming from a poplar
which shadows a right turn into the lane,
although no other tree has registered a breeze.

Coming in to Land

Twenty minutes out from Base we begin
a glide on course from ten thousand feet.
Up here it is warm in the sun, but we can see
on the ground it will be dull. Broken layers
of strato-cumulus are waste lands stretching

as far as the horizon; they are at two thousand,
and won't worry us for a while yet. We live
by death's negligence – I believe that, and think
of Don, though there is nothing to say; falling
short makes me despise myself. With airspeed

at 85 mph, the surging roar has ceased, and now
the old kite rests on the air slightly nose-down
and sighing. No vibration; both engines muted;
the props meandering round minute after minute
while the distant world imperceptibly approaches

with small clouds anchored like white Zeppelins
and flashing lakes and river-bends beyond them.
I never realised how much my life involved him –
things I remember seem endless, the whole region
is loaded and rich with them: Friesians lifting

their heads from grazing; cottage washing lines;
dust following a plough. All these sights become
less real and more as I know them. Shall I see Jean
when I'm home on leave? When Mrs. P let me know
Don had volunteered for airborne work overseas

I said "Jean will be sorry." But "Not sorry, proud"
came the answer; that soon brought me (betraying
my own youth) to youth's error: what if he's killed?
Here we go, sinking over the road, across the field,
skimming the hedge, and straight to the beginning

of the runway. It nears; it broadens; it rises
to become hard ground rushing past. Our engines
barely murmur, but we still rest on their air while grass
streams away on either side. At last comes the crunch
of first contact. We bounce a little and bump again –

bump (pause) bump, bump bump bump bump –
settling in quicker until we are easy. A grand life.
Sooner or later we shall come into line with the rest
and stop. Then the engines will cut, the props jerking
stickily to a halt. Then the silence will sing to me.

The Sin

In the same moment I bent to the amazing
adder snoozing on that sandy path ahead,
the landowner was shouting from the sun.

What are you doing? I would have explained,
but one obvious reason had already gone,
and there was no other. *Sir, not trespassing.*

A Dutch Interior

The dogs are a serious bore –
the pointer and the spaniel.
Their nails on the check floor
set painfully on edge
the teeth of each and everyone:
that stiffly standing page,

that dutiful and downcast girl,
and most of all that woman who
has recently uncurled
a message from its ribbon-ring,
read it twice, and now feels
all her strength departing.

A freshly whitewashed wall
behind her takes the weight;
stern morning sunlight pulls
her shadow to the dot of noon;
everything about her hesitates
but has to answer soon.

The dogs, however, they
already know. See that one there,
the pointer? Just the way
he crouches shows he's lost the will
to fight. The path is clear
and sweetly open for the spaniel.

The Stone

I have forgotten the sand
where I toppled onto my knees
and this immaculate stone
was suddenly snug in my hand.

Yes, I have forgotten the day,
the sun, the wind, the beach,
but not the look in your eye
when I took the stone away.

From the Journal of a Disappointed Man

I discovered these men driving a new pile
into the pier. There was all the paraphernalia
of chains, pulleys, cranes, ropes and, as I said,
a wooden pile, a massive affair, swinging

over the water on a long wire hawser.
Everything else was in the massive style
as well, even the men; very powerful men;
very ruminative and silent men ignoring me.

Speech was not something to interest them,
and if they talked at all it was like this –
"Let go," or "Hold tight": all monosyllables.
Nevertheless, by paying close attention

to the obscure movements of one working
on a ladder by the water's edge, I could tell
that for all their strength and experience
these men were up against a great difficulty.

I cannot say what. Every one of the monsters
was silent on the subject – baffled I thought
at first, but then I realised indifferent
and tired, so tired of the whole business.

The man nearest to me, still saying nothing
but crossing his strong arms over his chest,
showed me that for all he cared the pile
could go on swinging until the crack of Doom.

I should say I watched them at least an hour
and, to do the men justice, their slow efforts
to overcome their secret problem did continue –
then gradually slackened and finally ceased.

One massive man after another abandoned
his position and leaned on the iron rail
to gaze down like a mystic into the water.
No one spoke; no one said what they saw;

though one fellow did spit, and with round eyes
followed the trajectory of his brown bolus
(he had been chewing tobacco)
on its slow descent into the same depths.

The foreman, and the most original thinker,
smoked a cigarette to relieve the tension.
Afterwards, and with a heavy kind of majesty,
he turned on his heel and walked away.

With this eclipse of interest, the incident
was suddenly closed. First in ones and twos,
then altogether, the men followed. That left
the pile still in mid-air, and me of course.

The English Line

A belt of snow-flecked buddleia and elder;
the worn out cable/snake comparison;
ruins of a retaining wall with silver tag;

and crowning everything that Mute swan
flustering what has to be the Calder
in the likeness of a wind-hammered plastic bag.

Bright Star

When I had walked the circumference of the volcano
and heard the pitiful groans rising from its crater
as well as that quick, watery sound like roof-tiles
shattering on a marble pavement, I caught the train
back to my apartment in town and opened a bottle.

The earth was beautiful then, and the heavens too –
so much so, I uncapped my telescope and let myself
prowl for a while across the milky ranges, descending
at length through the smooth branches of a lemon tree
to one especially bright star which on closer inspection
turned out to be a lamp blazing on my neighbour's terrace.

Diagnosis

Twenty-one hours of daylight
now it's close to mid-summer,
and although most birds know
when to rest, posting themselves

like furtive love notes into the gaps
between stones in the harbour wall,
seagulls decide to tough it out,
rolling through the small hours

at head-height, too exhausted
to flap their wings or even feed.
The metal cries they give me,
starting another slow journey out

to Scapa Flow and back, mean
What do you want? Get some sleep.
My reply is to keep watching waves
slosh to and fro over the dead ships

as though they were the only things
to keep me awake here, which anyone
looking down from the granite hotel
and the road behind would also think,

since they cannot see you as I do, alive
in your illness and walking on the water,
but disappearing whenever the light shifts
and the sea beneath reveals itself again.

London Plane

They felled the plane that broke the pavement slabs.
My next-door neighbour worried for his house.
He said the roots had cracked his bedroom wall.
The Council sent tree-surgeons and he watched.
A thin man in the heat without a shirt.
They started at the top and then worked down.
It took a day with one hour free for lunch.
The trunk was carted off in useful logs.

The stump remained for two weeks after that.
A wren sat on it once.
Then back the tree-men came with their machine.
They chomped the stump and left a square of mud.
All afternoon the street was strewn with bits.
That night the wind got up and blew it bare.

The Benefit of the Doubt

The peregrine and the skylark
locked in a double suicide-dive
which could only end one way
found it continued in another.
I walk that country every day,

avoiding the abandoned shafts
which took them underground.
I choose my way very carefully.
I remember the stranger a thing
the less need to say as much.

The Grave of Rupert Brooke

In August 1969, when I had to accept
the temperature in Paris had died down,
my friends Mike and Sandy came with me

to Greece, hitching. We were seventeen.
Our first stop was Skyros, to find the grave
of the one poet I had read through entirely:

Rupert Brooke (his leather-bound *Collected
Poems*, a school prize, held pride of place
in my parents' book-whirligig at home) –

and although we did find what we wanted
at last, the effort and danger of that day
in 90 degrees with too little water, no hats,

and worn-out flip-flops to cover the whole
universe of trackless and razor-sharp lava
around Trebuki Bay, was quite literally

almost the end of us. At my lowest point
I hallucinated a flock of nanny goats
rolling down rocks like church bells

thrown from a steeple: it turned out
they were real. The grave might have been
a dream, too: English country churchyard

with railing painted a rainy green
and writing along the edge of the stone
saying Rupert Brooke had died defending

the city of Constantinople from the Turks.
I only remembered that later. At the time
I was transfixed by the army of red ants

marching from a crack in the coping.
Could those balls of dirt passing between
some of their many hands really be the last

remains of the poet? I kept such thoughts
to myself. I buried them deeper still
a week later at Delphi, where we drank

from the Castalian Spring, then pitched
camp under the olive trees overlooking
the Omphalos and waited for nightfall.

It would come quickly, we knew that,
and to make sure we missed nothing
lay down on our sleeping bags in silence,

sinking through sweet thyme and dust
as it cooled across limestone outcrops.
Next thing, I felt the gigantic mass

of the earth turning beneath me, solid
but ghostly, while my attention lifted
beyond the silver fringe of olive leaves

to the canopy of stars and shooting stars,
and beyond them into space expanding
forever, darkness beyond darkness,

while I shrank back into mere atoms,
on tenterhooks for the voice of prophesy
to break the hush and speak to me by name,

saying that my life counted for something,
or that I would be back home soon,
or at least that I would sleep safe tonight

underneath this enormous weight of sky,
with the ants and other small creatures
tickling over my hands and bare face

until the dew came and drove them away
underground or wherever else they might live,
and how that would be good enough for me.

The Cinder Path

I know what it means
to choose the cinder path.

You might say death
but I prefer taking

pains with the world.
The signpost ahead

which bears no inscription.
That elm tree withstanding

the terrible heat
of its oily green flame.

Geology

I had it from Fortey down in Trilobites,
who heard it from Oakley of Piltdown fame:
when our new appointment was confirmed
the Keeper himself flew like a raven
the whole length of the Museum cawing:

"We've got Bairstow! We've got Bairstow!"
Ah, Bairstow. The youngest Fellow at King's,
Cambridge, and a student of belemnites –
dull-looking fossils, frankly, but scattered
throughout the Lias which stands exposed

in cliffs and along the foreshore at Whitby.
Their chief value lies in the dating of levels,
and as for their interest – that is confined to
variations in size, some having the proportions
of a cheroot, others being closer to a Havana.

They are of course no more than the calcite
"guards" of small squid-like molluscs; remains
of the whole animal are hardly ever discovered.
But this was enough for Bairstow. In a career
spanning forty years he combed through the Lias,

collecting even the most miniature specimens
from each of its many layers, returning home,
and recording them by means of a unique system
developed entirely in isolation, which operated
with cards and knitting needles. After five years

his room was a maze. After fifteen a labyrinth.
Eventually – a web, with Bairstow at the centre
wearing thick green eyeshades, plying his needles.
I arrived with his retirement and we met only once,
when I took my courage in both hands and tip-toed

past his record books and stacks of loose paper,
his folders and files, and put to him a question
I now forget. Something about the Lias, like as not.
The truth is, I wanted simply to set my eyes on him,
and understand why he had never published a word.

I got my answer, since I could hardly fail to notice
he had carefully unpicked the string from every parcel
of specimens he had ever received, and preserved them
according to size in labelled boxes – viz: "two/three feet,"
"one/two feet," and "pieces too small to be of any use."

A Goodnight Kiss

When I come to the border around midnight
holding your amazingly light body in my arms,
your feet kick suddenly and we cross over.

There is your grandmother walking ahead of me
along a narrow ridge between the paddy fields
and *kiss-kiss* is the sound of her black sandals
making peace with the earth then taking leave of it.

Talk about Robert Frost

Did you ever hear Frost read?

Once, north of Boston,
in my final year. Some friends and I
had gone week-ending in the woods –
two days of reading, fending for ourselves,
and one professor sort of taking charge.
He'd known Frost from way back, and so Frost came.
Or blew in, rather, through the cabin door.

You must have thought...

I thought I'd seen the face of God –
Old Testament, of course: the windswept hair
the kindly-uncle face which might be harsh.
I couldn't tell what trouble he had known,
or how near death he was, he looked so...
Happy, I could say. Blithe is what I mean.

And he read what?

Extraordinary, familiar things. It made me think
of how a baker might pass round the loaves
he'd just pulled from the oven. Warm, they felt.

And that was all?

Not only that. As he read on, a storm brewed up
and filled the world behind him. Daylight failed;
wind dropped; the first few snow-buds blossomed
on the silver birch; and we could feel it drawing close –

Was Frost put off?

99

He never heard. But there,
behind him in the window, there it was.

And you?

We held our circle as we had to do,
all watching him, he thought, all keeping step
while he trod backwards through his own old snow,
and came and went through sundry other trees.
But losing him, in fact – some out to meet the storm,
some inwards, taking cover where we could.

Like him, you mean?

You could say that. Like him.
Except – I told you – he had no idea. Or none
until the weather reached us. Then he knew.

A Garden in Japan

Between crows at dawn
barking the latest news
of their Shogun ancestors

and sparrows at dusk
debating the meaning
of a fragile economy,

the International Garden
discovers a stillness
absolute as brushwork.

Slow carp might stir
the long lily roots
with their silk kimonos,

clouds will definitely
drag the odd shadow
across duckweed lawns,

but the one real event
will be my decision
to lift a red leaf

from the fang of rock
overhanging this pool,
and so free the current

to fall to earth
which will never again
be one and the same.

The View from Here

Sunk in the bottom right-hand corner
of the scene whichever way you look at it
is a blistered hulk of plain red brick
that could never be mistaken for a factory
but only seen for what it is: a prison.

The background is pure Middle of Nowhere –
a slope of pine trees scribbled over
by the gigantic wheels of logging trucks,
and shadows swung between pylons
on their march towards a white horizon.

The same goes for the river, or could it
be the mouth of an estuary? Either way,
there are enough stripped tree-trunks
penned at the edge of its slow current
to make a world-class library, or a shelf

for each household in the neighbourhood.
Though to judge by the look of things,
communication here is more a matter
of masts and dishes than faces and pages.
The wind has right of way on every street

except in the same right-hand corner
where a man in a parka, a Native American,
has found shelter to light his cigarette.
Perhaps he is visiting his friend in prison,
or finding a way home after his own release?

That is another thing not to be sure about,
like the time of day, since such flat greenness
could as well be dawn as midnight this far north.
Easy enough, on the other hand, to imagine
what crimes wait on the road into the distance

and what chances for love there might be
under the shelter of this hammered sky,
if someone patient were inclined to wait
for the small door in the prison wall to open,
so that later tonight two heads could lie

together on the same pillow and hear
the sound of their breathing hold its own,
along with the river grinding its wooden teeth,
wind raising its voice in the pylon wires, the sssh
of snow on the picture window turning to rain.

The Ancient Mariner

As our watch ended in the small hours
and the icebergs became visible again,
he floated alongside the weather leach
of the topsail, just above the yard-arm,
tilting his head sideways and glancing
along the bulging belly of the course.

"See what he's doing?" I said. "Taking a look
at the blunt-line and the clew-line lizards,
to see they're running clear and won't foul
if we have to fit up fast for the next squall."
To myself I thought: *Who's missing him?*
How long is it since he went overboard?

Cecelia Tennyson

Park House was always like a secret,
set on the north side of the valley
among beech woods, but overlooking
them and the main line from London

to Maidstone. Behind the narrow front
containing only a bare entrance hall,
stood another hall, much more likeable,
with a fine circular stone staircase rising

to the floor where Cecelia lived. Cecelia,
eleventh of the twelve Tennyson children,
whom I saw only for moments at a time
in the beginning of the new century. "Zilly,"

she said, tapping downstairs after tea
(and never before, whatever the weather),
"I'm out for a stroll." Zilly was my friend,
her only daughter – an old lady herself –

and knew the routines. On her way through
the larger hall with the view, Cecelia stopped
to stroke the bust of her first-born, Edmund,
who had died young, with a fastidious look

that might have been mistaken as a reproach
to idle dusting, except she spoke to the boy
very affectionately. Once I heard her say this:
"Tasso, I think, speaks of an infant's death

beautifully. I cannot recollect the words,
but it sipped the cup of life and perceiving
its bitterness turned its head and refused
the draught"; and on a different occasion –

and again, with no word of her Maker –
"A sorrow like ours can neither be increased
nor diminished by outward circumstances;
it has a life independent of them." Afterwards

she wandered outside into the gardens
where she would stray for twenty minutes.
Zilly and I looked aside then, but still waited
to be visible when she stepped back indoors,

always saying to Zilly, if it were winter-time,
in a deep, complaining and mournful voice,
"Very dark tonight." To which Zilly replied,
"Of course it is my dear. The sun has gone down."

The Old Head

We reached Louisburg after midnight
and woke next morning in a universe
of wonders: the post-box in the drive
was a post-box but emerald green.

And as for the fishermen's nets
crispy and stinking in the harbour,
the lobster pots like instruments
of torture for babies, the trawlers

unpronounceable with apostrophes...
I set about collecting each specimen
until, on the evening of that same day,
my decently hushed mother and father,

who also looked brand new to me –
and, to judge by their tact in walking
a yard apart, to each other as well –
decided a stroll in the twilight

would whet their appetite for dinner.
At the precise moment I imagined
they might link arms or otherwise
cross whatever it was between them,

they veered further apart, my mother
back to the hotel with her cardigan –
tied round her waist – unusual, that –
dropping into the dust, which spoiled

the effect, while my father's finger
beckoned me to the fuchsia hedge.
*Look at those deep reds! You don't
ever see that at home now, do you?*

The Break

Big-boned, red-faced children sprawl
exactly where I did and dangle
bacon rind to catch green crabs.

Nervous pincers pull their weight
an inch or so above the tide-scum
then plop back and magnify.

Nothing changes, nothing changes:
That's the message tapped in morse
by metal ropes on drawn-up boats.

It's all a lie. It's all a lie.
When I stroll past with my daughter
I no longer cast a shadow.

Hers has darkened as it should –
and look, the waking lighthouse lifts
a trumpet to its lips again.

Meeting at Night

I met my brother when he was sleepwalking.
We were back at school, on the top landing
outside his dormitory, and his gaze fell on me
like the indifferent moonlight. Why I was there
myself at that very late hour is still a mystery.

Feeling suddenly junior, I stole after him
to the wash-room, then paused in the doorway
marvelling as he drifted beside the ghostly basins
and reached the window overlooking the garden.
I could imagine the lawn shivering with dew,

the interference of cedar branches, and the lake
bulging like mercury under the taut night sky.
But as far as I could tell he was blind to all this.
When he eventually turned round I discovered
a look of such fear and sadness on his white face

I guessed that he had seen instead every one
of the sixty boys in the school, me included,
and the dozen tyrannical and hairy masters,
dead in their box-beds like meat at the butcher.
The next minute he pushed angrily past me

with no sign of recognition and floated off
down the blue lino to his dormitory again.
There he forgot to shut the door behind him,
but found his bed all right and turned himself
in a quick jangle of springs before lying still.

Raven

Crashing the hush of winter and midday –
the fire ablaze, but sunlight piling in
so flames look tissue or not there at all –
my father, in his Sunday best, appears
to interrupt me in the window-bay.
"What's this you're reading? Not *The Origin
of Species*?" I say, "Hardly, dad. *The Calls
of Common Birds*. You see? You want to hear?"

He settles down and I go mouthing off:
the barn owl's snore before its screech of pain;
the starling's click; the jay's fantastic joke;
the robin's "tic-tic-whee"; the raven's cough. . . .
But then he's interrupting me again,
"The raven's cough? You mean the raven's croak."

What Have We Here?

Dad got home late
and I never heard the gravel
or his door-clunk in the drive-through,
still less his shoeless step
as he crept to perch on my bedside.
"What have we here?"
It was a Yeomanry day,
and not even the thick whiskery cloth
of his battle-dress trousers
could blunt the edge of my *Ladybird* under the covers.

"Nelson, Dad." He squared his shoulders.
The order was, no reading after lights out,
so I was caught cold, like the polar bear
I'd just seen dispatched
in the pack ice off Spitzbergen.
On the other hand, Nelson was England's darling.
I'd seen that too, in the cockpit death scene
with Hardy's kiss on my forehead.
Dad checked a page, before his weight lifted and went.

I fell at once into a dream of *Victory* –
how she wallowed through Biscay
with sail-tatters smoking –
then gave my signal for a change of course.
At which she side-stepped her Channel-lane,
shimmied over the Hampshire hills,
rode the surge to London,
and made fast to a spire of Westminster
overlooking Trafalgar Square.

With that, the famous brandy barrel
burst its ropes at the main mast,
and the man himself slithered out

wizened and glistening as a fledgling,
but perfectly fit again.
He proved this by scaling the column
a grateful nation had raised for him,
and posed by his coil of rope
until he stiffened into stone.

Next morning, with dad in his City suit,
I snaffled his *Times* at breakfast
and rolled it into a telescope
so I could prove my grasp of history.
"What have we here?"
This time I couldn't answer.
The thing was pressed to my blind left eye,
and supposing I'd said "Your face"
he would know I was only inventing things.

Veteran

This visit to my father's house
ends with the two of us
side by side at his kitchen window
in silence, facing the old view.

Across the field, the wood
shudders under lilac cloud,
which a while ago was a bird
and is now a shroud,

draping the winter trees
with filigree rain-gauze:
a handful of sun flukes
gilding the drab trunks.

My father and I watch.
Are we about to catch
a burst of orange after-glow,
or will the evening go

headlong down to night?
With the sad weight
of a man dragging chains,
he has managed to remain

on track through his tour
of flashbacks from the war:
three fog-soaked years
of square-bashing and canvas;

the sick, flat-bottomed dash
of D day; the frothy wash
of waves inside his tank
as it declined to sink;

the hell-for-leather advance
when the lanes of France
shrank bottle-tight, blazing;
the ash-wreck of Berlin.

This is by heart, of course,
all at his own pace
now dust has settled again
and fear, grief, boredom, pain

have found out how to fade
into the later life he made.
But I still look at him –
the way his eyes take aim

and hold the wood in focus
just in case anonymous
and twilit-baffled trees
might in fact be enemies

advancing. I look up at him,
and cannot estimate the harm
still beating in his head
but hidden in his words.

What might he have done?
What might I have done,
frightened for my life,
to make my future safe?

Did he kill a man?
Did he fire the gun
with this crumpled finger
which now lifts and lingers

on the swimming glass,
and points out how the mass
of cloud above the wood
has melted from a shroud

into a carnival mask?
I never dare to ask.
I would rather not show
the appetite to know

how much of his own self
he shattered on my behalf.
He is my father, my father,
and from him all I gather

are things that he allows,
turning from the window
before the sinking sky
has buried the wood entirely

and telling him it's time
I headed off for home,
while he still stares outside
and waits for the parade

of shadow-shapes to end,
his slightly-lifted hand
either showing I should stay
or pushing me away.

Passing On

By noon your breathing had changed from normal
to shallow and panicky. That's when the nurse said
Nearly there now, in the gentle voice of a parent
comforting a child used to failure, slipping her arms
beneath your shoulders to hoist you up the pillows,
then pressing a startling gauze pad under your jaw.

Nearly there now. The whole world seemed to agree –
as the late April sky deepened through the afternoon
into high August blue, the vapour trails of two planes
converged to sketch a cross on the brow of heaven.
My brother Kit and I kept our backs turned to all that
except now and again. It was the room I wanted to see,

because it contained your last example of everything:
the broken metal window-catch that meant no fresh air;
your toothbrush standing to attention in its plastic mug;
the neutral pink walls flushed into definite red
by sunlight rejoicing in the flowering cherry outside;
your dressing-gown like a stranger within the wardrobe

eavesdropping. That should have been a sign to warn us,
but unhappiness made us brave, or do I mean cowardly,
and Kit and I talked as if we were already quite certain
you could no longer hear us, saying how easy you were
to love, but how difficult always to satisfy and relax –
how impossible to talk to, in fact, how expert with silence.

You breathed more easily by the time we were done,
although the thought you might have heard us after all,
and our words be settling into your soft brain like stones
onto the bed of a stream – that made our own breathing
tighter. Then the nurse looked in: *Nothing will change
here for a while boys*, and we ducked out like criminals.

116

I was ordering two large gins in the pub half a mile off
when my mobile rang. It was the hospital. You had died.
I put my drink down, then thought again and finished it.
Five minutes later we were back at the door to your room
wondering whether to knock. Would everything we said
be written on your face, like a white cross on the heavens?

Of course not. It was written in us, where no one could
        find it
except ourselves. Your own face was wiped entirely clean –
and so, with your particular worries solved, and your
        sadness,
I could see more clearly than ever how like mine it was,
and therefore how my head will eventually look on the
        pillow
when the wall opens behind me and I depart with my
        failings.

The Wish List

You also took these with you underground:
your check Viyella shirt; your regimental tie;

a too-late letter from your grandson, Jesse Mo;
your *Book of Common Prayer*. On second thoughts

make room for these things too: the china hare
I lifted from your bedside table years ago

and kept, to prove I loved you like a child;
your father's bone-backed hairbrushes

worn down to fuzz; the gilt Saint Christopher
you carried through the war; your army pack

for D day with its German phrase book and a map
of Normandy; your snaps of Berlin station

with the roof blown off; mum's wedding ring;
the yellow dress she wore on honeymoon;

your City suit; your bowler hat; your brolly
furled and dusted with dry flecks of rain;

your season ticket for the London train; your pen;
your leaving portrait with the twisting hands;

your hunting breeks; your crop; the Gammage cap;
a swallow bull's-eyed in the stable yard; your box

of fishing flies; your rod and net; your waders
hanging in the garage upside down; your pullover

118

with pockets bulged like fists; your specs;
your blotter scarred with hieroglyphs; your Bensons

and your TV guide; your *Telegraph*;
your diary with its pale blue empty pages;

your appointment card; your vase of floppy roses
Kit brought from the garden; your electric bell;

your stone-cold tea; your straw; your cardboard bowl;
your Kleenex box; your photograph of home;

your radio still cranking out *Today*; your dying word
which, though I held my breath, I never heard.

All Possibilities

My dead father, who never knew what hit him,
is taking his evening walk through the village.
My brother and I tag along too, kicking stones
at a respectful distance, also our Norfolk terrier,
and my mother in her hospital bed: that rasp-rasp
will be her iron wheels as they disturb the gravel.

His mood is bad. The war ended again this morning
and although he still won, it no longer feels that way.
How come the new town simmering on the horizon?
How come the blank faces and no one remembering
his name? The final straw arrives with the old park,
now a golf course, where his grandparents used to live.

With one hand he is already holding his walking stick
the wrong way round, ready to swing at buttercups;
with the other he shades his eyes and tries to make out
who is playing, and who are the ghosts of his ancestors.
They advance steadily through the twilight and threaten
to circle him, wearing the bright diamond sweaters.

"Fore!" he is shouting, to cover all possibilities. "Fore!"

The Mower

With storm light in the east but no rain yet
I came in from mowing my square of lawn
and paused in the doorway to glance round
at my handiwork and the feckless apple blossom

blurring those trim stripes and Hovver-sweeps
I had meant to last. What I saw instead was you
in threadbare cords, catching the sunny interval
between showers, trundling the Ransome out

from its corner in the woodshed. The dizzy whiff
of elm chips and oil. Joke-shop spider-threads
greying the rubber handles. Gravel pips squeaking
as the roller squashed through the yard. Then a hush

like the pause before thunder while you performed
your ritual of muffled curses and forehead wipes,
your pessimistic tugs on the starter cable,
more curses, more furious yanks, until at long last

the engine sulked, recovered, sighed a grey cloud
speckled with petrol-bits, and wobbled into a roar.
Off came the brake and off charged the machine,
dragging you down to the blazing Tree of Heaven

at the garden end, where the trick was to reverse
without stalling or scraping a hefty mud-crescent,
before you careered back towards Kit and me
at our place in the kitchen window, out of your way.

To and fro, to and fro, to and fro, to and fro,
and each time a few feet more to the left, sometimes
lifting one hand in a hasty wave which said *Stay put!*
but also *I'm in charge!*, although we understood

from the way your whole body lurched lopsided
on the turn, this was less than a hundred percent true.
Getting the job done was all we ever wanted,
parked with our cricket things and happy enough

to wait, since experience had taught us that after
you'd unhooked the big green metal grass-basket
splodged with its Royal Appointment transfer,
lugged it off to the smoking heap by the compost,

thumped it empty, then re-appeared to give us
the thumbs up, we were allowed to burst suddenly
out like dogs into the sweet air, measure the pitch
between our studious stump-plantings, toss to see

who went in first, then wait for you to turn up again
from the woodshed where you had taken five minutes
to switch the petrol off, and wipe the blades down,
and polish the grass basket although it never would

shine up much, being what you called venerable.
You always did come back, that was the thing.
As you also come back now in the week you died,
just missing the first thick gusts of rain and the last

of the giddy apple blossom falling into your footprints,
with bright grass-flecks on your shoes and trouser-legs,
carefree for the minute, and young, and fit for life,
but cutting clean through me then vanishing for good.

Acknowledgments

"A Dying Race," "In the Attic," and "Anniversaries" were first published in *The Pleasure Steamers* (Carcanet, Manchester, 1976).

"Anne Frank Huis" and "The Letter" were first published in *Secret Narratives* (Salamander Press, Edinburgh, 1983).

"Look" and "Hull" were first published in *Love in a Life* (Faber and Faber, 1991).

"To Whom It May Concern," "The Spoilt Child," "Tortoise," "Fresh Water," "Goethe in the Park," "On the Table," and "Glen Ellen Stories" were first published in *Salt Water* (Faber and Faber, 1997).

"Mythology," "Great Expectations," "On the Island," "Serenade," "A Glass of Wine," "The Fox Provides for Himself," and "In Memory of Elizabeth Dalley" were first published in *Public Property* (Faber and Faber, 2002).

"The Life of William Cowper," "Coming in to Land," "From the Journal of a Disappointed Man," "The Ancient Mariner," and "Cecelia Tennyson" are all varieties of the "found" poem, and use material from the following: *Selected Letters of William Cowper*, ed. William Hadley (1926); *The Unreturning Spring* by James Farrar (1968); *The Journal of a Disappointed Man* by W. N. P. Barbellion (1919); *Birds Britannica*, ed. Mark Cocker and Richard Mabey (2005); and *The Tennysons: Background to Genius* by Charles Tennyson and Hope Dyson (1974). "Harry Patch" uses some phrases from *The Last Fighting Tommy* by Harry Patch with Richard Van Emden (2007).

ABOUT THE AUTHOR

ANDREW MOTION was born in London, England, on October 26, 1952. He studied English literature at University College, Oxford University, and wrote about the poetry of Edward Thomas for an M. Litt. He taught English literature at the University of Hull and creative writing at the University of East Anglia. He was editor of *Poetry Review* (1981–1983), and editorial director and poetry editor at London publishers Chatto & Windus (1983–1989).

He was awarded the Newdigate Prize at Oxford for his poem "Inland," included in his first collection of poems, *The Pleasure Steamers*, published in 1977; since then, he has published ten books of poetry. He is also the author of several acclaimed biographies including *The Lamberts: George, Constant, and Kit* (1986), which won a Somerset Maugham Award; *Philip Larkin: A Writer's Life* (1993 UK edition, 1993 US), which won the Whitbread Biography Award; and *Keats: A Biography* (1997 UK edition, 1998 US). His memoir, *In the Blood: A Memoir of My Childhood*, was published in Great Britain in 2006, and in the United States by David R. Godine in 2007.

An acclaimed poet, critic, biographer, and lecturer, Andrew Motion was appointed the British Poet Laureate in May 1999, succeeding Ted Hughes. He lives in London, where he is a Fellow of the Royal Society of Literature.

A NOTE ON THE TYPE

The Mower *has been set in Minion, a type designed by Robert Slimbach in 1990. An offshoot of the designer's researches during the development of Adobe Garamond, Minion hybridized the characteristics of numerous Renaissance sources into a single calligraphic hand. Unlike many faces developed exclusively for digital typesetting, drawings for Minion were transferred to the computer early in the design phase, preserving much of the freshness of the original concept. Conceived with an eye toward overall harmony, its capitals, lower case, and numerals were carefully balanced to maintain a well-groomed "family" appearance – both between roman and italic and across the full range of weights. A decidedly contemporary face, Minion makes free use of the qualities Slimbach found most appealing in the types of the fifteenth and sixteenth centuries. Crisp drawing and a narrow set width make Minion an economical and easygoing book type, and even its name reflects its adaptable, affable, and almost self-effacing nature, referring as it does to a small size of type, a faithful or devoted servant, and a kind of peach.*

DESIGN & COMPOSITION BY CARL W. SCARBROUGH